50
of the most
witty,
acerbic
& erudite
things
ever said about
Money

HARRIMAN HOUSE LTD
43 Chapel Street
Petersfield
Hampshire
GU32 3DY
GREAT BRITAIN

Tel: +44 (0)1730 233870
Fax: +44 (0)1730 233880
Email: enquiries@harriman-house.com
Website: www.harriman-house.com

First published in Great Britain in 2002, reprinted in 2006
Copyright Harriman House Ltd
Published by Harriman House Ltd
The right of Philip Jenks to be identified as the author has been asserted
in accordance with the Copyright, Design and Patents Act 1988.

ISBN: 1-897-59797-5
ISBN 13: 9-781897-597972

British Library Cataloguing in Publication Data
A CIP catalogue record for this book can be obtained from the British Library.

Printed and bound by Biddles Ltd, Kings Lynn, Norfolk

Contents

First principles

The nature of investing

What it is

"Although it's easy to forget sometimes, a share of a stock is not a lottery ticket. It's part ownership of a business."

Peter Lynch, legendary manager of The Magellan Fund

"Speculation is an effort, probably unsuccessful, to turn a little money into a lot. Investment is an effort, which should be successful, to prevent a lot of money becoming a little."

Fred Schwed, author of 'Where are The Customers' Yachts?'

How you win at it

"It's not whether you're right or wrong that's important, but how much money you make when you're right and how much you lose when you're wrong."

George Soros

"People who look for easy money invariably pay for the privilege of proving that it cannot be found on this sordid earth."

Edwin Lefevre, author of 'Reminiscences of a Stock Operator'

"The market, like the Lord, helps those who help themselves. But, unlike the Lord, the market does not forgive those who know not what they do."

Warren Buffett, CEO of Berkshire Hathaway

What it takes to succeed

"The list of qualities an investor ought to have include patience, self-reliance, common sense, a tolerance for pain, open-mindedness, detachment, persistence, humility, flexibility, a willingness to do independent research, an equal willingness to admit mistakes, and the ability to ignore general panic."

Peter Lynch

"You don't need to be a rocket scientist. Investing is not a game where the guy with the 160 IQ beats the guy with the 130 IQ."

Warren Buffett

Risk

"If no one ever took risks, Michelangelo would have painted the Sistine floor."

Neil Simon, playwright

"October is one of the peculiarly dangerous months to speculate in stocks. Other dangerous months are July, January, September, April, November, May, March, June, December, August and February."

Mark Twain

"The ultimate risk is not taking a risk."

Sir James Goldsmith

"It's one of the ironies of investing. The rich can afford to take risks, but don't need to. The poor need to take risks, but often can't afford to."

Jonathan Clements

Time

"The best time to invest is when you have money. This is because history suggests it is not timing which matters, but time."

Sir John Templeton

"The best time to plant a tree was twenty years ago. The second best time is now."

Anon

"Compound interest."

Albert Einstein's reply, when asked to name man's greatest invention

"It is often said that the Indian who sold Manhattan Island in 1626 for $24 was rooked by the white man. In fact he may have been an extremely sharp salesman. Had he put his $24 away at 6 per cent interest, compounded semi-annually, it would now be worth more than $50 billion, and with it his descendants could buy back much of the now-improved land."

Burton Malkiel, author of "A Random Walk Down Wall Street"

Buying shares

General guidelines

Be careful

"Select stocks the way porcupines make love - very carefully."

Bob Dinda

"There are more fools among buyers than among sellers."

French proverb

Simplicity

"Never invest in any idea you can't illustrate with a crayon."

Peter Lynch

"I don't try to jump over 7-foot bars. I look around for 1-foot bars that I can step over."

Warren Buffett

Concentrate on companies, not the market

"Playing the stock market is analogous to entering a newspaper beauty-judging contest in which one must select the six prettiest faces out of a hundred photographs, with the prize going to the person whose selections most nearly conform to those of the group as a whole."

John Maynard Keynes

"John Maynard Keynes essentially said, don't try and figure out what the market is doing. Figure out a business you understand, and concentrate."

Warren Buffett

"If you remember nothing else about P/E ratios, remember to avoid stocks with excessively high ones. A company with a high P/E must have incredible earnings growth to justify its high price."

Peter Lynch

"Things are seldom what they seem. Skim milk masquerades as cream."

Gilbert and Sullivan, playwrights, verse from 'H.M.S. Pinafore'

The 'efficiency of markets' theory

"I'd be a bum on the street with a tin cup if the markets were efficient ... Investing in a market where people believe in efficiency is like playing bridge with someone who has been told it doesn't do any good to look at the cards."

Warren Buffett

"I have noticed that everyone who ever told me that the markets are efficient is poor."

Larry Hite

"The more the theory of efficient markets is believed, the less efficient the markets become."

George Soros

The qualities of good companies

Understanding what they do

"Draw a circle around the businesses you understand and then eliminate those that fail to qualify on the basis of value, good management and limited exposure to hard times."

Warren Buffett

Straightforward businesses

"I like buying companies that can be run by monkeys - because one day they will be."

Peter Lynch

"In a difficult business, no sooner is one problem solved than another surfaces - never is there just one cockroach in the kitchen."

Warren Buffett

Good fundamentals?

"When management with a reputation for brilliance tackles a business with a reputation for poor fundamentals, it is the reputation of the business that remains intact."

Warren Buffett

Products in continuing demand

"If you can find a company that can get away with raising prices year after year without losing customers (an addictive product such as cigarettes fits the bill), you've got a terrific investment."

Peter Lynch

"You go to bed feeling very comfortable just thinking about two and a half billion males with hair growing while you sleep. No one at Gillette has trouble sleeping."

Warren Buffett

but . . .

"The FTSE 100 index is a collection of yesterday's success stories. It says nothing about tomorrow."

Guy Manson

Market strength

"The race is not always to the swift, nor the battle to the strong, but that's the way to bet."

Damon Runyon

"If you gave me $100 billion and said take away the soft drink leadership of Coca-Cola in the world, I'd give it back to you and say it can't be done."

Warren Buffett

"Don't buy market leaders. Find a #7 company in an industry headed for the #3 spot because its recognition increases and its P/E expands. There's more money to be made in finding tomorrow's winners than in chasing yesterday's."

Foster Friess, CEO, Brandywine Funds

"The best assurance of continued growth, and high profit margins, comes back to this: the company should have a special niche in the marketplace, so that sales don't depend on offering a commodity item at a lower price than the competition's. It should, to a degree, dominate that niche. The best company in a marginal industry is worth more than the third-best company in a major industry. I'd rather own the shares of Hokuto, the leading mushroom grower in Japan, than of Mitsubishi Motor or Subaru."

Ralph Wanger, CEO, The Acorn Funds

Not capital intensive

"Never invest your money in anything that eats or needs repainting."

Billy Rose, New York showman

Frugal management

"I got positive feelings when I saw that Taco Bell's headquarters was stuck behind a bowling alley. When I saw those executives operating out of that grim little bunker, I was thrilled. Obviously they weren't wasting money on landscaping the office."

Peter Lynch

The difference between price and value

"What is a cynic? A man who knows the price of everything and the value of nothing."

Oscar Wilde

"For some reason people take their cues from price action rather than from values. Price is what you pay. Value is what you get."

Warren Buffett

"It's far better to buy a wonderful company at a fair price, than a fair company at a wonderful price. Now, when buying companies or common stocks, we look for first-class businesses accompanied by first-class managements."

Warren Buffett

Value investing

Margin of safety

"I put heavy weight on certainty. It's not risky to buy securities at a fraction of what they're worth."

Warren Buffett

"Ben Graham wasn't about brilliant investments and he wasn't about fads of fashion. He was about sound investing, and I think sound investing can make you very wealthy if you're not in too big of a hurry. And it never makes you poor, which is even better."

Warren Buffett

Value investors have to be patient

"If Graham was alive today, he might argue that you should simply withdraw from the market for a few years until conditions arise which offer you value for money that you are seeking. Graham might be right, but my problem is that I would get so bored waiting."

Jim Slater, legendary UK growth investor

Earnings must be predictable

"I look for businesses in which I think I can predict what they're going to look like in ten to fifteen years time. Take Wrigley's chewing gum. I don't think the internet is going to change how people chew gum."

Warren Buffett

A mood of pessimism can be good for value investors

"The most common cause of low prices is pessimism - sometimes pervasive, sometimes specific to a company or industry. We want to do business in such an environment, not because we like pessimism but because we like the prices it produces. It's optimism that is the enemy of the rational buyer."

Warren Buffett

"Value stocks have another attraction: they are constantly in fresh production. A new batch often appears when the troubles of a few leaders taint a whole industry."

Ralph Wanger

"The word 'crisis' in Chinese is composed of two characters: the first, the symbol of danger . . . the second, of opportunity."

Anon

Contrarian investing

"The crowd always loses because the crowd is always wrong. It is wrong because it behaves normally."

Fred Kelly, author of 'Why You Win or Lose'

"Conventional wisdom results in conventional returns."

Mario Gabelli

"There is a very important difference between being a theoretical contrarian and dealing with it in practical terms."

Michael Steinhardt, Wall Street money manager

"Investors may be quite willing to take the risk of being wrong in the company of others, while being much more reluctant to take the risk of being right alone."

John Maynard Keynes

Small caps and growth stocks

"Elephants don't gallop."

Jim Slater, explaining why he prefers small cap shares

"Buy the stocks of small companies below their economic value, let the companies grow, and resell them as proven successes at full economic value. Individuals often sell small companies below their economic value and buy mature companies at full value, thus providing the other side for our trades."

Ralph Wanger

"Small is good, micro is not. For the littlest companies, it's like auditioning for the chorus line: one misstep and you're out. I've made it a practice to stay away from the start-ups, the tiny techs, the near-venture-capital situations. I want companies that are established and whose management have proven, at least thus far, that they know how to run a company."

Ralph Wanger

"When people ask how we've managed to get our results, I tell them it's not by avoiding disasters, because I have had my fair share of them. That's understood with small cap investing. But if you manage to own some stocks that go up ten times, that pays for a lot of disasters, with profits left over."

Ralph Wanger

"There are few worse investments than a growth share going ex-growth."

Jim Slater

Technology stocks

"Our reaction to a fermenting industry is much like our attitude toward space exploration: we applaud the endeavour but prefer to skip the ride. Obviously many companies in high-tech businesses or embryonic industries will grow much faster than will The Inevitables [like Coca-Cola and Gillette]. But we would rather be certain of a good result than hopeful of a great one."

Warren Buffett

"Technology companies should be valued at a discount to the shares of companies like Disney and Coca-Cola, which have long term earnings."

Bill Gates

"Were there a direct relationship between technological innovation and investment results, then equity returns in the first half of the 19th century should have been spectacular. Alas, they were not. History shows that it is precisely the promise of unlimited technological progress that proves most corrosive to equity returns."

Bill Bernstein, CEO of efficientfrontier.com

"There seems to be an unwritten rule on Wall Street: If you don't understand it, put your life savings into it. Shun the enterprise round the corner, which can at least be observed, and seek out one that manufactures an incomprehensible product."

Peter Lynch

"If I could avoid a single stock, it would be the hottest stock in the hottest industry, the one that gets the most favourable publicity, the one that every investor hears about in the car pool or on the commuter train - and, succumbing to the social pressure, often buys."

Peter Lynch

"Since the Industrial Revolution began, going downstream - investing in businesses that will benefit from new technology rather than investing in the technology companies themselves - has often been the smarter strategy."

Ralph Wanger

"Glamour has nothing to do with a niche's appeal. A dull business run by a good businessman is far better than a glamorous business with mediocre management. And even if the glamorous business is run by a genius, often, in that kind of industry, its competitors are also geniuses, so nobody has an advantage, as I've commented about high-tech companies."

Ralph Wanger

"We have embraced the 21st century by entering such cutting-edge industries as brick, carpet, insulation and paint. Try to control your excitement."

Warren Buffett

"If you want to be entertained, take up skydiving. There's an inverse correlation between an investment's entertainment value and its expected return."

Bill Bernstein

Researching companies

The necessity for research

"Investing without research is like playing poker without looking at the cards."

Peter Lynch

"Great stocks are extremely hard to find. If they weren't, then everyone would own them."

Philip A. Fisher, author of 'Common Stocks & Uncommon Profits'

Reports and accounts

Many investors ignore them

"Most men would rather die than think. Many do."

Bertrand Russell

...at their peril

"Hollow vessels make the greatest sound."

Anon

"When you buy a stock for its book value, you have to have a detailed understanding of what those values really are. At Penn Central, tunnels through mountains and useless rail cars counted as assets."

Peter Lynch

"A fully fledged economic downturn will cause nastier things to come out of the woodwork. The old market saying is: 'Recessions uncover what auditors do not.'"

Philip Coggan, Financial Times columnist

"If you're considering a stock on the strength of some specific product that a company makes, the first thing to find out is: what effect will the success of the product have on the company's bottom line?"

Peter Lynch

But don't take them at face value

"Statistics are like prisoners under torture: with the proper tweaking you can get them to confess to anything."

John Rothchild, author of 'Survive & Profit in Ferocious Markets'

"Statistics are like a bikini. What they reveal is suggestive, but what they conceal is vital."

Aaron Levenstein

"Never pay the slightest attention to what a company president ever says about his stock."

Bernard Baruch

"It is one of my assumptions in reading accounts that the finance directors of PLCs are rarely stupid, so that any change in accounting treatment or wording, or simply any specific form of words used, is likely to have a purpose and it is as well that we know what it is."

Terry Smith, author of 'Accounting for Growth'

You don't need to be an expert

"Read Ben Graham and Phil Fisher, read annual reports, but don't do equations with Greek letters in them."

Warren Buffett

"I was a lousy accountant. I always figured that if you came within eight bucks of what you needed you were doing OK. I made the difference up out of my own pocket."

Bob Newhart

Cash and debt

"A company that descends into loss making often succeeds in making a comeback. One which runs out of cash (and friends) rarely has a second chance."

Alan Sugden, 'Interpreting Company Reports & Accounts'

"Debt isn't good, debt isn't bad. To put it in the extreme, for some companies no debt is too much leverage. For others a debt of 100% can easily be absorbed. People assume the capital structure of a company is burned in stone. The capital structure, like the individual, is constantly changing."

Michael Milken, junk bond svengali at Drexel Burnham Lambert

Quality of management

Are their interests aligned with yours?

"I like the directors to own a number of shares substantial enough to give the 'owner's eye', but not so many that they have control, can sit back and could at some stage block a future bid. I like to see a good cross-section of the directors with reasonable shareholdings and I always worry if the Finance Director is not among them."

Jim Slater

Are they driven?

"Our prototype for occupational fervour is the Catholic tailor who used his small savings of many years to finance a pilgrimage to the Vatican. When he returned, his parish held a special meeting to get his first-hand account of the Pope. "Tell us," said the eager faithful, "just what sort of fellow is he?" Our hero wasted no words. "He's a forty-four medium.""

Warren Buffett

"Whenever I read about some company undertaking a cost-cutting program, I know it's not a company that really knows what costs are about. The really good manager does not wake up in the morning and say "This is the day I'm going to cut costs," any more than he wakes up and decides to practise breathing."

Warren Buffett

The danger of a loss of focus

"Loss of focus is what most worries Charlie [Munger] and me when we contemplate investing in a business that looks outstanding. All too often, we've seen value stagnate in the presence of hubris or boredom that caused the attention span of managers to wander. Would you believe that not a few decades back they were growing shrimp at Coke and exploring for oil at Gillette?"

Warren Buffett

"All those ego-feeding activities - the long hours in the limousine, the sky-larking in the corporate jet, the collection of press clippings, the unnecessary speeches - feed the corporate sickness and one way or another make a corporate problem out of what had been an otherwise perfectly competent, even brilliant executive."

Harold Geneen, then boss of ITT

Results aren't the whole story

"Good management to Wall Street means nothing more than a company with three consecutive quarters of rising earnings. Make it four quarters and you have great management. But exciting performance numbers by themselves aren't enough to qualify managers as superior, at least not in my book. One good year or two could be a fluke. Or maybe current management's predecessors set operations up so well that the incumbents haven't had time to wreck everything."

Ralph Wanger

Competitors as a source of information

"Managements can be guarded, especially if they know we own a lot of their stock. But their competitors will usually talk freely about them. It's like trying to find out about a young lady you are interested in. If you ask her mother, you are certainly going to get a different perspective than you would if you asked the boyfriend she has broken up with. We like to hear what the boyfriend has to say."

Ralph Wanger

"I read annual reports of the company I'm looking at and I read the annual reports of the competitors - that is the main source of material."

Warren Buffett

Inside information and tips

Against

"There is something about inside information which seems to paralyse a man's reasoning powers."

Bernard Baruch

"Wall Street professionals know that acting on 'inside tips' will break a man more quickly than famine, pestilence, crop failure, political readjustments or what may be called normal accidents."

Edwin Lefevre

"With enough inside information and a million dollars you can go broke in a year."

Warren Buffett

"The tips that pay off sufficiently overshadow the poor overall results for publishers to make a good living out of it. But not, according to my previous calculations, their subscribers."

Mike Mitchell, publisher of TipTracker

For

"Anybody who plays the stock market not as an insider is like a man buying cows in the moonlight."

Daniel Drew, 19th century speculator

Research from professional analysts

"Investors are slow to learn that security analysts do not always mean what they say."

Hersh Shefrin

"Either they're trying to con you or they're trying to con themselves."

Warren Buffett

"Enron: Strong buy"

The rating maintained by Richard Gross, analyst at Lehman Brothers, as Enron's stock declined from $81 to $0.75. A Lehman spokesperson helpfully explained to the New York Times that the firm was advising Dynegy on its purchase of Enron's pipeline, and it was Lehman's policy not to change the firm's rating on any company involved in a deal in which Lehman was an adviser.

Portfolio management

Diversification

For

"Why look for the needle in the haystack? Buy the haystack!"

John Bogle, CEO ,The Vanguard Funds, arguing the case for index-tracking funds

Against

"Diversification may preserve wealth, but concentration builds wealth."

Warren Buffett

"Diversification is a hedge for ignorance. I think you are much better off owning a few stocks and knowing a great deal about them."

William J. O'Neil, author of 'How to Make Money in Stocks'

"As time goes on, I get more and more convinced that the right method in investment is to put fairly large sums into enterprises which one thinks one knows something about and in the management of which one thoroughly believes. It is a mistake to think that one limits one's risk by spreading too much between enterprises about which one knows little and has no reason for special confidence."

John Maynard Keynes

Buy-and-hold

The Buffett view

"All there is to investing is picking good stocks at good times and staying with them as long as they remain good companies."

Warren Buffett

"My favorite time frame for holding a stock is forever."

Warren Buffett

"I never attempt to make money on the stock market. I buy on the assumption that they could close the market the next day and not reopen it for five years."

Warren Buffett

"If the job has been correctly done when a stock is purchased, the time to sell it is - almost never."

Philip A. Fisher

Pay no attention to short-term price movements

"As far as I am concerned, the stock market doesn't exist. It is only there as a reference to see if anybody is offering to do anything foolish."

Warren Buffett

"You do better to make a few large bets and sit back and wait. There are huge mathematical advantages to doing nothing."

Charlie Munger

What about active traders?

"According the name 'investors' to institutions that trade actively is like calling someone who repeatedly engages in one-night stands a romantic."

Warren Buffett

A different viewpoint: the dangers of buy-and-hold

"Buy and hold is far from the sure thing it's made out to be. It works in bull markets. It works if you invest in dribs and drabs, catching the ups and downs along the way. It works in mild bear markets, when declines are quickly reversed. It *may* work if you've got 20 years to wait for stock to recover from a half-off sale. Otherwise, it's risky. It's risky when you're holding stocks you bought at extravagant prices. It's extremely risky when your retirement depends on a positive result and you're planning to take up golf in a decade or less."

John Rothchild

Movement of share prices

Sentiment counts in the short term

"That stocks rise and fall on corporate earnings is a much ballyhooed misconception. The price investors will pay for earnings varies from hour to hour, week to week, year to year depending on the inclinations of the buyers and the sellers."

John Rothchild

"Share prices follow the theorem: *hope* divided by *fear* minus *greed*."

Dominic Lawson

Earnings count in the the long term

"In the short run, the market is a voting machine. In the long run, it's a weighing machine."

Warren Buffett

"If the business does well, the stock eventually follows."

Warren Buffett

"Just because the price goes up doesn't mean you're right. Just because it goes down doesn't mean you're wrong. Stock prices often move in opposite directions from the fundamentals but long term the direction and sustainability of profits will prevail."

Peter Lynch

Ultimately, investment returns are tied to corporate returns

"Stocks can't outperform businesses indefinitely. Indeed, because of the heavy transaction and investment management costs they bear, stockholders as a whole and over the long term must inevitably underperform the companies they own. If American business, in aggregate, earns about 12% on equity annually, investors must end up earning significantly less. Bull markets can obscure mathematical laws, but they cannot repeal them."

Warren Buffett

How important is monetary liquidity?

"In the stock market, as with horse racing, money makes the mare go. Monetary conditions exert an enormous influence on stock prices. Indeed the monetary climate - primarily the trend in interest rates and Federal Reserve policy - is the dominant factor in determining the stock market's major direction."

Martin Zweig, author of 'Winning on Wall Street'

"If Fed Chairman Alan Greenspan were to whisper to me what his monetary policy was going to be over the next two years, it wouldn't change one thing I do."

Warren Buffett

Other factors

"The thing that most affects the stock market is everything."

James Palysted Wood

Bull & bear markets

Bull markets flatter to deceive

"Bull markets go to people's heads. If you're a duck on a pond, and it's rising due to a downpour, you start going up in the world. But you think it's you, not the pond."

Charlie Munger

"You must never confuse genius with a bull market."

Nick Leslau, property entrepreneur

No-one likes bears

"If you warn 100 men of possible forthcoming bad news, 80 will immediately dislike you. And if you are so unfortunate to be right, the other 20 will as well. "

Anthony Gaubis

"A bear in a bull market is like a prohibitionist at a cocktail party. At first, some people take his admonitions to heart and sip soda water. But as the party goes on, nearly everyone joins in the drinking. Scorned, scoffed at, and - worst of all - ignored, the prohibitionist slips out to await the morning after."

Jeffrey Laderman

"It's no accident that the largest investment house in the world, Merrill Lynch, has a bull for a mascot, and took 'Bullish on America' for its corporate motto. No investment house has dared adopt the slogan 'Bearish on America', even during market declines. Pessimists have a hard time making a living in America."

John Rothchild

"Outperform your peers in a bull market and you'll be applauded for your skill. Outperform them in a bear market - by turning a profit when they're nursing losses - and check your backside for darts, your rose bushes for poison, and your driveway for nails. On Wall Street a winning bear gets more cold shoulder than an SEC gumshoe."

John Rothchild

Why do bear markets happen?

"Bear markets happen for a simple reason: the owners of the merchandise can't get their asking price. The shortage of buyers forces them to lower the fare, until a buyer can be coaxed into making a deal. It's a common occurrence in retail. Stores have a bear market after every Christmas rush."

John Rothchild

The frequency of bear markets

"Nasty bear markets happen every six and a half years. Smaller declines of 10 per cent, called 'corrections', happen every two years or so. Taken together, these minor and major setbacks have produced losses in thirty-three years out of the past one hundred, making investors unhappy roughly one-third of the time."

John Rothchild

Bear tracks

"A bear market is a financial cancer that spreads. Intermediate rallies (occasionally very strong ones) keep the hopes of investors alive. Furthermore, by continuously publishing bullish reports, brokers and economists, like good nurses, keep the flame of hope from burning out. But after 18 to 36 months of continued losses, total capitulation usually sets in and a major low occurs."

Marc Faber

"Markets don't go straight down. They go down hard, get oversold, rally, then go down again."

Byron Wein

But what an opportunity!

"Like an oversexed guy in a whorehouse. This is the time to start investing."

Warren Buffett, when asked by *Forbes* in October 1974, at the bottom of the bear market, how he felt.

"The 1973-1974 collapse, brought the capitalization of the British market down to a mere $50 billion. This was less than the yearly profits of the OPEC oil-producing nations, whose increase in oil prices contributed to the decline in share values. The OPEC nations could have purchased a controlling interest in every publicly traded British corporation at the time with less than one year's oil revenues!"

Jeremy Siegel, author of 'Stocks for the Long Run'

Scars from a bear mauling

"Nobody who has ever been on a falling elevator and survived ever approaches such a conveyance without a fundamentally reduced degree of confidence."

Robert Reno, analyst and writer, after the 1987 crash

"Markets can remain irrational longer than you can remain solvent."

John Maynard Keynes

Timing the markets

Fantastic! – if you can do it

"The key to building wealth is to preserve capital and wait patiently for the right opportunity to make the extraordinary gains."

Victor Sperandeo, author of '*Trader Vic*'

But very few can

"No mutual fund manager who relies on market timing has kept his job for fifteen years. Individual investors who try to time the market will be tossed on the same horns."

Ralph Wanger

"In the 30 years in this business, I do not know anybody who has done it successfully and consistently, nor anybody who knows anybody who has done it successfully and consistently. Indeed my impression is that trying to do market timing is likely not only not to add value to your investment program, but to be counterproductive."

John Bogle

Most private investors get it the wrong way round

"Too many people redeem their profits too quickly. In a huge bull market they wind up with piddling profits, only to watch their former holdings soar. That usually prompts them into making mistakes later when, believing that the market owes them some money, they buy at the wrong time at much higher levels."

Martin Zweig

"Most people get interested in stocks when everyone else is. The time to get interested is when no one else is. You can't buy what is popular and do well."

Warren Buffett

Everyday signs of a market top or bottom

"When you see business execs helicoptering to the golf course, waiters discussing the merits of Intel versus Applied Materials, 22-year-olds in suspenders smoking cigars and drinking. Martinis, and houses in the suburbs selling way over the asking price - then you know that the referee has brought the whistle to his lips and is about to blow. The game is nearly over."

James K. Glassman

"When 10 people would rather talk to a dentist about plaque than to the manager of an equity mutual fund about stocks, it's likely that the market is about to turn up. When the neighbours tell me what to buy and I wish I had taken their advice, it's a sure sign that the market has reached a top and is due for a tumble."

Peter Lynch

"When the ducks quack, feed them" (trad. Wall St. saying)

"Without doubt, the most striking feature of the financial era which ended in the Autumn of 1929 was the desire of people to buy securities, and the effect of this on values. But the increase in the number of securities to buy was hardly less striking. And the ingenuity and zeal with which companies were devised in which securities might be sold was as remarkable as anything."

John K. Galbraith

When to sell

No hard and fast rules

"Some people automatically sell the 'winners' - stocks that go up - and hold on to their 'losers' - stocks that go down - which is about as sensible as pulling out the flowers and watering the weeds. Others automatically sell their losers and hold on to their winners, which doesn't work out much better. Both strategies fail because they're tied to the current movement of the stock price as an indicator of the company's fundamental value."

Peter Lynch

Cutting losses

"Take care to sell your horse before he dies. The art of life is passing losses on."

Robert Frost, poet

"Long term investments are short term investments which have gone wrong."

Anon

"There is no such thing as a paper loss. A paper loss is a real loss."

Jim Rogers, former partner of Soros in the Quantum Fund

"If you know why you bought a stock in the first place, you'll automatically have a better idea of when to say goodbye to it."

Peter Lynch

"I always sell on the first profit warning. Wait til the third downgrade and you have no hope of getting out."

Nicola Horlick, fund manager

Running profits

"You can't make five or ten or twenty times your money if you don't hold on to stocks. Most people are delighted when a stock doubles, and quickly sell to lock in their gain. If a company is still performing, let its stock, too, continue to perform."

Ralph Wanger

"I made my money by selling too soon."

Bernard Baruch

"You can never go broke by taking a profit."

Meyer Rothschild

Selling in a bear market

"An investor in a panicky market faces the same predicament as a movie-goer in a crowded theater after somebody shouts "Fire!" Staying put is the sensible thing to do, as long as everybody else stays put and stays calm. Otherwise, people who stay put run the risk of getting trampled, and people who rush to the exit may have the best chance of escape."

John Rothchild

"Selling an illiquid stock in a down market brings to mind the galley slaves in Ben-Hur, chained to their bench while the ship sinks."

Ralph Wanger

New issues

"The entire financial industry exists to sell a product. If you don't understand this basic maxim, you'll be misled time after time."

Timothy Vick, investment manager at Arbor Capital

"The new issue market is ruled by controlling stockholders and corporations who can usually select the timing of offerings. Understandably these sellers are not going to offer any bargains. It's rare you'll find X being sold for half-X. Indeed, selling shareholders are often motivated to unload only when they feel the market is overpaying."

Warren Buffett

"The IPO market is never in equilibrium. It's either too hot or too cold. Buy in the cold periods."

Jay Ritter, Professor of Finance, University of Florida

Fund managers

Who needs 'em?

"If you can tell the difference between good advice and bad advice, you don't need advice."

Anon

"Twenty years in this business convinces me that any normal person using the customary 3% of the brain can pick stocks as well as, if not better, than the average Wall Street expert."

Peter Lynch

"Full-time professionals in other fields, let's say dentists, bring a lot to the layman. But in aggregate, people get nothing for their money from professional money managers."

Warren Buffett

"Having a financial adviser enables the investor to carry a psychological call option. If the investment decision turns out well, the investor takes the credit, and if it turns out badly, the regret can be lowered by blaming the adviser."

Hersh Shefrin

The fund manager mindset

"In the world of investment management, it is far better to fail very badly in a conventional way and lose a great deal of money for your client than to lose a little in an unconventional fashion."

Marc Faber

"Whoever imagines that the average Wall Street professional is looking for reasons to buy exciting stocks hasn't spent much time on Wall Street. The fund manager most likely is looking for reasons not to buy exciting stocks, so that he can offer the proper excuses if those exciting stocks go up."

Peter Lynch

"Between the chance of making an unusually large profit on an unknown company and the assurance of losing only a small amount on an established company, the normal mutual-fund manager, pension-fund manager, or corporate-portfolio manager would jump at the latter. Success is one thing, but it's more important not to look bad if you fail."

Peter Lynch

Their salaries and your returns

"If you pay the executives at Sara Lee more, it doesn't make the cheesecake less good. But with mutual funds, it comes directly out of the batter."

Don Phillips, President of Morningstar, Inc.

Performance of active funds

"How can institutional investors hope to outperform the market when, in effect, they are the market?"

Charles Ellis, author of 'Winning the Loser's Game'

"One of the trends we have found is that the fund managers that tend to perform the best over time are the ones that tend to spend the least amount of time debating which way the market is heading."

Don Phillips, Morningstar, Inc.

"One of the ironies of the stock market is the emphasis on activity. Brokers, using terms such as 'marketability' and 'liquidity', sing the praises of companies with high share turnover. But investors should understand that what is good for the croupier is not good for the customer. A hyperactive stock market is the pickpocket of enterprise."

Warren Buffett

"One reason why bubbles swell up and go pop is that investment managers all puff and blow at the same time."

Christopher Fildes, writer for Spectator magazine

"The management of stock exchange investments is a kind of low pursuit from which it is a good thing for most members of society to be free."

John Maynard Keynes

Short-term trading

Key axioms

"Trading has been, and always will be, a hard way to make an easing living."

Jeffrey Silverman

"The elements of good trading are cutting losses, cutting losses and cutting losses."

Ed Seykota

"The price that people agree to in the pit is not the price that people think is going to exist in the future. It's the price that both sides vehemently agree won't be there."

Jeffrey Silverman

"If a man is both wise and lucky, he will not make the same mistake twice. But he will make any one of ten thousand brothers or cousins of the original. The mistake family is so large that there is always one of them around when you want to see what you can do in the fool-play line."

Edwin Lefevre

Mechanical systems

"If you are either a conservative or a very nervous investor, a mechanical system might be smart. It certainly achieves two goals: it limits potential losses and it helps you sleep at night. As for maximizing your returns, I think that's another story."

Jonathan Steinberg

"A good bet is that all systems will stop working when you use them."

Victor Niederhoffer, author of 'The Education of a Speculator'

"It is inconceivable that anyone will divulge a truly effective get-rich scheme for the price of a book . . . There is ample opportunity to use wealth in this world, and neither I nor my friends, nor anyone else I have ever met, has so much of it that they are interested in putting themselves at a disadvantage by sharing their secrets."

Victor Niederhoffer

"Investing in stocks is an art, not a science, and people who've been trained to rigidly quantify everything have a big disadvantage."

Peter Lynch

"There is no sadder sight in the world than to see a beautiful theory killed by a brutal fact."

Thomas Huxley

Disciplined risk management

"There are old traders around and bold traders around, but there are no old, bold traders around."

Bob Dinda

"The only time I really ever lost money was when I broke my own rules."

Jesse Livermore, legendary trader

"I think appreciating risk, being aware of it and respecting it, makes you a good trader. It teaches you to be disciplined. Discipline allows you to trade effectively. You can take your ego out of it. You can go wrong 60, 70 percent of the time and still make a lot of money. If you ignore the discipline of managing risk, you have to be right 80 percent of the time or more, and I don't know anyone who's that good."

Larry Rosenberg

Activity / inactivity

"Throughout all my years of investing I've found that the big money was never made in the buying or the selling. The big money was made in the waiting."

Jesse Livermore

"Losing traders are typically hooked even stronger than successful traders by virtue of the intermittent nature of the reward. My cat follows me into the kitchen every time I go, yet not once in ten times does he get his turkey snack reward. I suspect that this behavior is practically impossible to extinguish."

Jeffrey Silverman

A cynic's view of charting

"The technicians do not help produce yachts for the customers, but they do help generate the trading that produces yachts for the brokers."

Burton Malkiel

"Many sceptics, it is true, are inclined to dismiss chart reading as akin to astrology or necromancy; but the sheer weight of its importance in Wall Street requires that its pretensions be examined with some degree of care."

Benjamin Graham

The emotional aspect of trading

"I do the opposite of what I feel I should do - When I'm sick in my stomach, it's time to buy. When I feel great, it's time to sell."

Elaine Gazarelli, US fund manager famed for calling the 1987 Crash

"The person who knows that he doesn't know much, knows much."

Marc Faber

"When you're feeling manic, you've got to develop the discipline to recognize the internal signs and take the money. And when you're feeling depressed, you've got to avoid jumping out the basement window and buy the market."

Jeffrey Silverman

"Deciding on an investment philosophy is like picking a spouse. Do you want someone who is volatile, romantic and emotional, or do you want someone who is steady and trustworthy and down to earth. If you want a successful investment career, you'd better bind yourself to a style you can live with."

Ralph Wanger

"If you can't control your emotions, being in the market is like walking into a heated area wearing a backpack full of explosives."

Charles Ellis

Deals and Dealmakers

The urge to merge

"Chief executives seem no more able to resist their biological urge to merge than dogs can resist chasing rabbits."

Philip Coggan, Financial Times columnist

"When a chief executive officer is encouraged by his advisors to make deals, he responds much as would a teenager boy who is encouraged by his father to have a normal sex life. It's not a push he needs."

Warren Buffett

"Dealmaking beats working. That's why there are deals that make no sense."

Peter Drucker

"In the search for companies to acquire, we adopt the same attitude one might find appropriate in looking for a spouse: it pays to be active, interested, and open-minded, but it does not pay to be in a hurry."

Warren Buffett

"I like deals where two plus two can equal five. If you can only get it to equal three-and-a-half, you might as well stay in bed."

Fred Johnston, newspaper tycoon

The Art of the Deal

"Negotiation is the art of letting the other side have your way."

Daniel Vare, Italian diplomat

"When someone says "it's not about money", it's about money."

H. L. Mencken

"You can get a lot more done with a kind word and a gun than with a kind word alone."

Al Capone, entrepreneur

"The big print giveth, and the small print taketh away."

Bishop Fulton J. Sheen

"You don't understand Joe. I'm not here for an interview."

Carl Icahn, corporate raider, when challenged by a Morgan Stanley banker representing Phillips Petroleum "What the hell do you know about the oil business?"

The importance of the 'exchange rate' in paper deals

"A company that wants to use its own stock as currency for an acquisition has no problems if the stock is selling in the market at full intrinsic value. But suppose it is selling at only half intrinsic value. In that case it is faced with the unhappy prospect of using a substantially undervalued currency to pay for a fully valued property [the negotiated price of the target company]. In effect the acquirer must give up \$2 of value to receive \$1 of value. Under such circumstances, a marvellous business purchased at a fair sales price becomes a terrible buy. For gold valued as gold cannot be purchased intelligently through the utilization of gold valued as lead."

Warren Buffett

two + two = *what?*

"Many mergers turn out to be monumental stinkers, with the acquired company sold after an enormous write-off. Putting two drunks together doesn't make a stable person."

Gary Hamel

"Too many mergers resemble the marriage of two cripples who become twice as old, twice as bureaucratic and twice as undynamic."

Peter Drucker

Mergers as a defensive measure

"As incumbents seek to increase the concentration of industry power, newcomers plot ways to dilute it. While dinosaurs merge, upstarts race toward the future. Bulk is no bulwark against the onslaught of revolutionary new competitors. And it's hard to mate and run at the same time."

Gary Hamel

Ethics and governance

Executive share options

"An executive who hedges his stock options is like the captain of a ship who sees an iceberg up ahead and heads for his lifeboat without waking the sleeping passengers."

Business Week, on the device known as a zero-cost collar, by which executives protect the value of their stock options against a slide in their company's share price

Reputation

"It takes 20 years to build a reputation and five minutes to ruin it. If you think about that, you'll do things differently."

Warren Buffett

"Ratner's has got very little to do with quality. We do cut-glass sherry decanters with six glasses on a silver-plated tray - and it only costs 4.95. People say how can you sell this for such a low price. I say because it's total crap."

Gerald Ratner, describing his company's products to an audience at The Institute of Directors, 1991

Corporate donations

"Many corporate managers deplore governmental allocation of the taxpayer's dollar but embrace enthusiastically their own allocation of the shareholder's dollar to charities of their own choosing. We've yet to find a CEO who believes he should personally fund the charities favored by his shareholders. Why, then should they foot the bill for his picks?"

Warren Buffett

Non-executive directors

"Like bidets, you're not quite sure what they're for, but they add a touch of class."

Michael Grade, on the role of non-execs

"It's an old joke, but worth retelling that emeritus is a Latin word. 'E' means he's out and 'meritus' means he deserved it."

Neil Bennett, on Iain Vallance's 'chairman emeritus' title at BT

Crime and scams

Plus ça change, plus c'est la meme chose

"Behind every great fortune, there is a crime."

Honore de Balzac

"There are no new forms of financial fraud; in the last hundred years there have only been small variations on a few classic designs."

J. K. Galbraith

"Long periods of prosperity usually end in scandal."

George Taucher

"Thieves respect property. They merely wish the property to become their property that they may more perfectly respect it."

G. K. Chesterton

But he's normally such a *good* boy

"There is perhaps no record of a bank fraud existent of which the perpetrator was not honest yesterday."

James S. Gibbons

"The thing I would most like to see invented is a way of teaching children and grown-ups the difference between right and wrong."

Robert Maxwell

"The louder he talked of his honour, the faster we counted our spoons."

Ralph Waldo Emerson

In mitigation

"I was always working in the best interests of the bank."

Nick Leeson, Barings' 'rogue trader'

"Everything we had was in Enron stock. We are struggling for liquidity."

Linda Lay, wife of Enron CEO Kenneth Lay, giving a tearful interview on the Today program. Reporters soon noted that the Lays had $8 million in stock in other companies and $25 million in property assets.

"Just because you're at the scene of an accident doesn't mean you caused it."

John Ormerod, managing partner of Andersen UK, on the firm's disastrous entanglement with Enron

Amateurs

"In white collar situations, they don't think of themselves as thorough-going criminals, so when they get caught there's a level of guilt involved. Suddenly there is a conflict between what they appear to families, friends, co-workers, and what they are doing in the secret part of their life. It tends to move them towards confessing, putting it all behind them. They haven't acquired the ethics of organised crime which is that you never help the government, constantly trying to frustrate it."

Rudolph Giuliani, former Mayor of New York City

"Organized crime in America takes in over forty billion dollars a year. That is quite a profitable sum, especially when you consider that the Mafia spends very little on office supplies."

Woody Allen

So what?

"No apologies to anybody, for anything. Apologies don't mean shit. What happened, happened."

John Gutfreund, who resigned from Salomon Brothers following a scandal in the bond market

"It is morally wrong to allow a sucker to keep his money."

W.C. Fields

"If we close a bank every time we find an example or two of fraud we would have rather fewer banks."

Robin Leigh-Pemberton, former governor of the Bank of England

Yes, it pays

"Money is the fruit of evil, as often as the root of it."

Henry Fielding

Banking

Banking crises

"A bank lives on credit. Till it is trusted it is nothing; and when it ceases to be trusted it turns to nothing."

Walter Bagehot

"Because we're independent, people come to us when they're in trouble. They come to auntie and auntie helps them. They find us wise, sympathetic and helpful - but not rich."

George Blunden, then Deputy Governor of the Bank of England

"Good bankers, like good tea, can only be appreciated when they are in hot water."

Jaffar Hussein, Governor, Malaysian Central Bank

Lenders

"A bank is a place where they lend you an umbrella in fair weather and ask for it back when it begins to rain."

Robert Frost

"Americans are still reasonably parochial. They'd rather make a bad loan in Texas than a good loan in Brazil."

Walter Wriston

"If you don't have some bad loans you are not in business."

Paul Volcker, former head of the Federal Reserve

"It is unanimously and without qualification assumed that when anyone gets into debt, the fault is entirely and always that of the lender and not the borrower."

Bernard Levin, journalist

"You can't run a Church on Hail Marys."

Archbishop Marcinkus, former head of the Vatican Bank

Borrowers

"If you want to know the value of money, try to borrow some."

Benjamin Franklin

"Debt is the slavery of the free."

Publius Syrus

Status and power

"Banking establishments are more dangerous than standing armies."

Thomas Jefferson

"A banker need not be popular. Indeed, a good banker in a healthy capitalist society should probably be much disliked."

John K. Galbraith

"I would rather see finance less proud and industry more content."

Sir Winston Churchill

"Goldman Sachs. Sounds like some kind of brothel, but I'm assured it's not."

Stephen Fry, presenting the Euromoney Awards in 2001

"When I was young, people called me a gambler. As the scale of my operations increased I became known as a speculator. Now I am called a banker. But I have been doing the same thing all the time."

Sir Ernest Cassel, private banker to King Edward VII

Political economy

"In this state of imbecility, I had, for my own amusement, turned my attention to political economy."

Thomas De Quincey, 'Confessions of an Opium Eater'

Economic policy

"All the great economic ills the world has known this century can be directly traced back to the London School of Economics."

N.M. Perrera

"I think there are two areas where new ideas are terribly dangerous - economics and sex. By and large, it's all been tried before, and if it's new, it's probably illegal or unhealthy."

Felix Rohatyn

"Without economy none can be rich and with it few will be poor."

Samuel Johnson

"You will live badly, but not for long."

President Alexander Lukaskenko of Belarus, the last European dictator, boosting his subjects' morale in 1998

"Waiting for supply-side economics to work is like leaving the landing lights on for Amelia Earhart."

Walter Heller, economist

Inflation

"Money is lacking? Well then, create it!"

Goethe

"The road to inflation is paved with good intentions."

William Guttmann

"Inflation is a great moral evil. Nations which lose confidence in their currency lose confidence in themselves."

Lord Howe, former Chancellor of the Exchequer

"Inflation might be called prosperity with high blood pressure."

Arnold Glasgow

"Central bankers are against inflation like priests are against sin. But few are out and out fundamentalists."

Guy Quaden, banker

"We have a love hate relationship. We hate inflation, but we love everything that causes it."

William Simon, banker

"Inflation is a form of taxation that can be imposed with legislation."

Milton Friedman, economist

"Inflation is worse than communism."

Robin Leigh-Pemberton, former Governor of the Bank of England

"Inflation isn't an Act of God. High inflation is a man-made disaster, like Southern beer and nylon shirts."

Ronald Long, consultant and professional Northerner

"Having a little inflation is like being a little bit pregnant."

Leon Henderson

Currencies and exchange rates

"Lenin was right. There is no subtler, no surer, means of overturning the existing basis of society than to debauch the currency."

John Maynard Keynes

"I want the whole of Europe to have one currency; it will make trading much easier."

Napoleon Bonaparte

The Sterling crisis of 1992

"The market thought the ERM was fundamentally weak. It wouldn't have mattered if you had Jesus Christ as Chancellor."

Doug Bate

"I could have made things more difficult but I didn't because I felt a certain responsibility not to destroy the European Monetary System."

George Soros

"It is just as if Norman Lamont had personally thrown entire hospitals and schools into the sea all afternoon."

Central Banking magazine

"If governments do try to fix the currency it is the duty of the currency speculators to blow them apart. By doing that, they would do the world a very good turn."

Martin Taylor, former CEO of Barclays Bank

"My approach works not by making valid predictions but by allowing me to correct false ones."

George Soros

Economists

Economists

"An economist is someone who will know tomorrow why the things he predicted yesterday didn't happen today."

Lawrence J. Peter, author of 'The Peter Principle'

"I want a one-armed economist so that the guy could never make a statement and then say "but on the other hand . . .""".

Harry S. Truman

"There are three kinds of economists. Those that can add, and those that can't."

Hamish McRae

"If all the economists were laid end to end they still wouldn't reach a conclusion."

George Bernard Shaw

"An economist is someone who sees something working in practice and asks whether it would work in principle."

Stephen M. Goldfeld

"The experience of being proved completely wrong is salutory. No economist should be denied it, and none are."

J.K. Galbraith

"Grow your own dope - plant an economist."

Graffiti seen at London School of Economics

Economic forecasting

"Forecasting is like trying to drive a car blindfolded and following directions given by a person looking out of the back window"

Anon

"There are two things you are better off not watching in the making: sausages and econometric estimates."

Edward Leaner

Oh yeah?

"Stock prices have reached a permanently high plateau."

Irving Fisher, economist, a few weeks before the 1929 crash

"Not a bear among them."

Barron's, Jan 1973, summing up the opinion of institutional investors at the onset of the biggest bear market in 36 years

"In a market like this, every story is a positive one. Any news is good news. It's pretty much taken for granted now that the market is going to go up."

Wall Street Journal, 26 Aug 87, the day after the market peak

Business and economic Cycles

"When your neighbour loses his job, it's a slowdown; when you lose your job, it's a recession; when an economist loses his job, it's a depression."

Anon

"As times get harder, words grow more weaselly. Euphemisms boom in a recession, even if nothing else does."

Alison Eadie

"You can't expect to see calves running in the field the day after you put the bulls to the cows, but I would expect to see some contented cows."

Calvin Coolidge, U.S. President, discussing the lack of results in the economy with Herbert Hoover

"We have gone from boom to bust faster than at any time since the oil shock. When you screech to a halt like that, it feels like getting thrown through the windshield."

Stephen S. Roach, Chief Economist of Morgan Stanley, on the dotcom meltdown in 2000

Dotcoms and Other Manias

When companies sought to raise capital at the time of the South Sea Bubble in 1720, they had to state the purposes to which the capital would be applied. Below are some examples which would have made even the founders of Boo.com blush.

'For trading in hair'

'For furnishing funerals to any part of Great Britain'

'For insuring to all masters and mistresses the losses they may sustain by servants'

'For improving the art of making soap'

'For a wheel of perpetual motion'

'For importing walnut trees from Virginia'

'For paving the streets of London'

'For drying malt by hot air'

'For extracting silver from lead'

'For buying and fitting out ships to suppress pirates'

Way out in front for sheer chutzpah comes this gem:

'For carrying on an undertaking of great advantage, but nobody to know what it is'

Why, oh why?

"All nations with a capitalist mode of production are seized periodically by a feverish attempt to make money without the mediation of the process of production."

Karl Marx

"I can calculate the motions of the heavenly bodies, but not the madness of people."

Sir Isaac Newton, who sold out profitably during the South Sea Bubble but was tempted back in and lost £20,000

"The only thing men learn from history is that men learn nothing from history."

Hegel

"Basic economic theory suggests that demand falls as prices go up. But in the case of speculative markets, the opposite seems to be true."

Marc Faber

"I think a lot of people initially thought that the 'e' in e-business was more important than the 'business'."

Michael Dell, billionaire founder of Dell Computer Inc.

"The speculative mania that was hyped in the net rivaled any previous bubble - including the one in 1620 with tulips. It separated a heck of a lot of people from their capital. And it did so permanently. It wasn't just a matter of share prices deviating from value, but rather, in many cases of share prices disappearing and not reappearing."

Mason Hawkins

True believers

"Yellowspan."

Chief Investment Strategist, WFBS Securities, baiting Alan Greenspan after the Fed Chairman had said the markets were being driven by 'irrational exuberance'.

"These are excellent results."

Chris Gent, CEO of Vodafone, in Vodafone's 2002 annual report which included a record $19.8bn loss

Alright for some

"For me, the richness is in the learning."

Allan Leighton, remarking on the continuing fall in value of his shareholdings in
lastminute.com

"Hopefully, investors learned that stocks have risks, especially start-ups in capital-intensive industries."

Jack Grubman, the $20 million a year telecoms analyst, whose recommendations lost
some investors 75% of their capital

"We are not a stock that you can sleep well with at night. We are a volatile stock . . . For a short-term investor, or for a small investor, I wouldn't invest in internet stocks."

Jeff Bezos, founder of Amazon.com

"Rail travel at high speed is not possible because the passengers, unable to breathe, would die of asphyxia."

Dr Dionysus Lardner, Professor of Natural Philosophy and Astronomy at University College, London

"This 'telephone' has too many shortcomings to be seriously considered as a means of communication."

Western Union internal memo, 1876, when turning down the offer of Bell's patents for $100,000

"Edison's ideas are good enough for our Transatlantic friends, but unworthy of the attention of practical or scientific men."

Report of a Committee set up by Parliament to look into Edison's work on the incandescent lamp, 1878

"Everything that can be invented has been invented."

Charles H. Duell, Director of the U.S. Patent Office, 1899, advising on the future need for a patent office

"The horse is here to stay. The automobile is only a fad."

Lawyer, explaining to Henry Ford in 1903 why he would not invest in the Ford Motor Company

"For God's sake go down to the reception and get rid of the lunatic down there. He says he's got a machine for seeing by wireless! Watch him - he may have a razor with him."

Editor of the Daily Express, faced with a visit by John Logie Baird, 1925

"Who the hell wants to hear actors talk?"

Harry M. Warner, CEO of Warner Brothers, on the commercial viability of talking pictures, 1927

"I think there is a market for about five computers."

Thomas J. Watson, Chairman of IBM, 1943

"The concept is interesting and well-formed, but in order to earn better than a 'C', the idea must be feasible."

Yale University professor, grading Fred Smith's paper proposing an overnight delivery service. Smith ignored him and went on to found Federal Express

"640k ought to be enough for anybody."

Bill Gates, 1981

Tax

"The hardest thing in the world to understand is income tax."

Albert Einstein

"The art of taxation consists in plucking the goose to obtain the largest amount of feathers with the least amount of hissing."

Jean-Baptiste Colbert, finance minister to Louise XIV

"The avoidance of taxes is the only intellectual pursuit that still carries any reward."

John Maynard Keynes

"The one thing that hurts more than having to pay income tax is not having to pay income tax."

Thomas Duwar

"We don't pay taxes. The little people pay taxes."

Leona Helmsley, hotel tycoon's wife, jailed for tax fraud

"In this world nothing is certain but death and taxes."

Benjamin Franklin

"There is just one thing I can promise you about the outer-space programme - your tax-dollar will go further."

Werner von Braun

"A tax loophole is something that benefits the other guy. If it benefits you, it's tax reform."

Russell Long, American politician

"Please note that we do not recruit tax specialists."

Inland Revenue web site, 2002

Money and life

Money and happiness

"When I was young I used to think that money was the most important thing in life. Now that I am old, I know it is."

Oscar Wilde

"Money can't buy you happiness, but it does bring you a more pleasant form of misery."

Spike Milligan

"Money is better than poverty, if only for financial reasons."

Woody Allen

"What's the use of happiness? It can't buy you money."

Henry Youngman

"Money, it turns out, is exactly like sex. You think of nothing else if you don't have it and think of other things if you do."

James Baldwin

"I'd like to live like a poor man with lots of money."

Pablo Picasso

"Poor people have more fun than rich people, they say. But I notice it's the rich people who keep saying it."

Jack Paar

"I wouldn't mind going to jail if I had three cellmates who played bridge."

Warren Buffett

"Having more money does not ensure happiness. People with ten million dollars are no happier than people with nine million dollars."

Hobart Brown

The value of money

"People's wealth and worth are very rarely related."

Malcolm Forbes

"The chief value of money lies in the fact that one lives in a world in which it is overestimated."

H. L. Mencken

Money and power

"Where money talks, there are few interruptions."

Herbert V. Prochnow

"Money is a terrible master but an excellent servant."

P. T. Barnum

"With money in your pocket, you are wise, and you are handsome, and you sing well too."

Jewish proverb

"When you win, you eat better, you sleep better, your beer tastes better, and your wife looks like Gina Lollobrigida."

Johnny Pesky, American baseball champion

Selling your soul to money

"If you marry for money, you will earn it."

Ezra Bowen

"It's important to me that money not be important to me."

Les Brown

Getting rich

First rungs

"Small opportunities are often the beginning of great enterprise."

Demosthenes

"I worked my way up from nothing to a state of extreme poverty."

Groucho Marx

"There were times when my pants were so thin, I could sit on a dime and tell if it were heads or tails."

Spencer Tracy

"To open a business is easy; to keep it open is very difficult. "

Chinese proverb

"It isn't enough for you to love money - it's also necessary that money should love you."

Baron Rothschild

"To turn $100 into a $110 is work. To turn $100 million into $110 million is inevitable."

Edgar Bronfman, President of Seagram Company

"The trouble, Mr Goldwyn is that you are only interested in art and I am only interested in money."

George Bernard Shaw, playwright, turning down Samuel Goldwyn's offer to buy the screen rights of his plays

"The meek shall inherit the earth, but not the mineral rights."

J. Paul Getty

The Lucky Sperm Club

"Nobody talks more of free enterprise, of competition and of the best man winning than the man who inherited his father's farm."

C. Wright Mills

"Inherited wealth is a big handicap to happiness. It is as certain death to ambition as cocaine is to morality."

William Vanderbilt

"Money - the one thing that keeps us in touch with our children."

Giles Brandreth

"Saving is a very fine thing. Especially when your parents have done it for you."

Sir Winston Churchill

"I did not marry my wife because she had four million. I would have married her if she had only two million."

Charles Forte, founder of the Forte hotel chain

Free Enterprise

"The entire essence of America is the hope to first make money, then make money with money, then make lots of money with lots of money."

Paul Erdman, author of 'The Crash of 79'

"The optimist sees opportunity in every danger; the pessimist sees danger in every opportunity."

Sir Winston Churchill

"If I had thought about it, I wouldn't have done the experiment. The literature was full of examples that said you can't do this."

Spencer Silver, on the work that led to 3-M's 'Post-It' notepads.

"There are few ways in which a man can be more innocently employed than in getting money."

Samuel Johnson

"Opportunity is missed by most people because it is dressed in overalls and looks like work."

Thomas Edison

"Buy land. They're not making it any more."

Mark Twain

"When it comes time to hang the capitalists they will compete with each other to sell us the rope at a lower price."

Lenin

"It is a socialist idea that making profits is a vice; I consider the real vice is making losses."

Sir Winston Churchill

"When you are skinning your customers, you should leave some skin on to grow so that you can skin them again."

Nikita Khrushchev

"Every successful enterprise requires three men - a dreamer, a businessman, and a son of a bitch."

Peter McArthur

"There is only one boss. The customer. And he can fire everybody in the company, from the chairman on down, simply by spending his money somewhere else."

Sam Walton, founder of Wal-Mart

"Catch a man a fish, and you can sell it to him. Teach a man to fish, and you ruin a wonderful business opportunity."

Karl Marx

"I'm all for unions, but we don't need them."

Ross Perot, during one of the regular confrontations between his company, EDS, and the Teamsters Union

"My God, you'll never believe the sort of money there is in running libraries."

Anonymous business reporter from a London newspaper, cabling his editor after interviewing Andrew Carnegie

"Most everything I've done I've copied from someone else."

Sam Walton

Venture Capital

"A lot of people become pessimists from financing optimists."

C.T. Jones

"Each time, it's a nice little company, nice people, modestly successful. Then you bring in the VC money - it's like putting jet engines on a VW. They expect that, within a year and a half, they will get back ten times their money . . . It runs up against the laws of physics. It's like putting nine women together and trying to make a baby in one month."

Dennis Faust

"Men who don't take risks won't drink champagne."

Russian saying

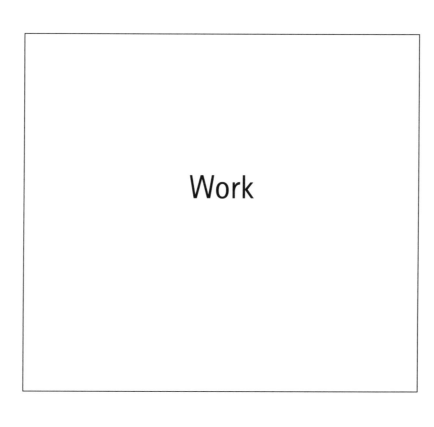

"It's probably true that hard work never killed anyone, but I figure why take the chance."

Ronald Reagan

"All paid employments absorb and degrade the mind."

Aristotle

"The only place where success comes before work is in the dictionary."

Vidal Sassoon

"Luck is a dividend of sweat. The more you sweat, the luckier you get."

Ray Kroc, founder of MacDonalds

"There are two kinds of people, those who do the work and those who take the credit. Try to be in the first group; there is less competition there."

Indira Gandhi

"Don't go around saying the world owes you a living. The world owes you nothing. It was here first."

Mark Twain

"Every day I get up and look through the Forbes list of the richest people in America. If I'm not on it, I go to work."

Robert Orben

"I like work. It fascinates me. I can sit and look at it for hours."

Jerome K. Jerome

"In all labor there is profit."

Proverbs 14:21

Being rich

Are you rich?

"A wealthy man is one who earns $100 more than his wife's sister's husband."

H. L. Mencken

"A billion dollars isn't what it used to be."

Nelson Bunker Hunt, whose family incurred debts of $1.8bn after failing to corner the silver market in the 1980s

"Let's get it clear on what phenomenal wealth is. I think that what Larry Ellison and Bill Gates have is phenomenal wealth. I'm just a two-bit billionaire."

Jim Clarke, founder of Silicon Graphics, Netscape and Healtheon

"A billion here, a billion there and pretty soon you're talking about real money."

Everett Dirksen

"If you can actually count your money, then you are not really a rich man."

J. Paul Getty

Being rich

"If you want to know what God thinks of money, just look at the people he gave it to."

Dorothy Parker

"I don't think it's terribly interesting how much money I give to charity because I have not solved any diseases yet. Until you do, what difference does it make?"

Larry Ellison, founder and CEO of Oracle

"Give me the luxuries of life and I will gladly do without the necessities."

Frank Lloyd Wright

"Do you know the only thing that gives me pleasure? It's to see my dividends coming in."

John D. Rockefeller

"The two days I have been happiest were when I bought my yacht and when I sold it. It was like a bottomless pit, although the crew got a lot of enjoyment out of it."

George Reynolds, safe-breaker and chipboard magnate

"With all the unrest in the world, I don't think anybody should have a yacht that sleeps more than twelve."

Tony Curtis, lines from 'Some Like it Hot'

"I am opposed to millionaires, but it would be dangerous to offer me the position."

Mark Twain

The anguish of the rich

"Nothing is more admirable than the fortitude with which millionaires tolerate the disadvantages of their wealth."

Rex Stout

"It's so expensive to be rich."

Susan Gutfreund, wife of John Gutfreund, then boss of Salomon Brothers

"I get so tired of listening to one million dollars here, one million dollars there. It's so petty."

Imelda Marcos

"I must say that I do wrestle with the amount of money I make, but at the end of the day what am I gonna say? I took less so that Rupert Murdoch could have more?"

Tom Hanks, on coming to terms with his $20 million-per-picture fee

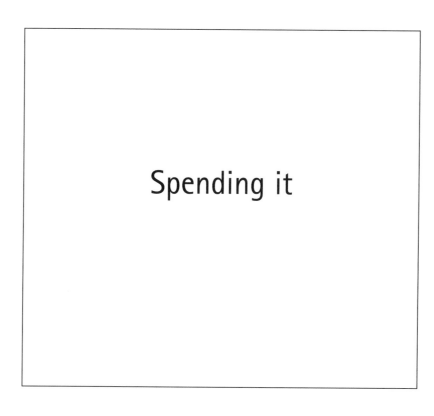

Spending it

"One of the dumbest things you can do with money is spend it."

Robert Wilson

"I don't know where the money went - it just went. I don't even like shopping."

The Duchess of York

"It's easier to create money than to spend it."

Warren Buffett

"I haven't reported my missing credit card to the police because whoever stole it is spending less than my wife."

Ilie Nastase

"I'm living so far beyond my income that we may almost be said to be living apart."

e.e. cummings, poet

"Sex is one of the most wholesome, beautiful and natural experiences that money can buy."

Steve Martin

"If money was meant to be held on to, they would have made it with handles."

old poker saying

"They say I wasted my money. I say 90% went on women, fast cars and booze. It was the rest I wasted."

George Best

"Whoever said money can't buy happiness didn't know where to shop."

Gertrude Stein

"If women didn't exist, all the money in the world would have no meaning."

Aristotle Onassis

"A man is a person that will pay two dollars for a one dollar item he wants. A woman will pay one dollar for a two dollar item she doesn't want."

William Binger

"Money can't buy happiness; it can, however, rent it."

Anon

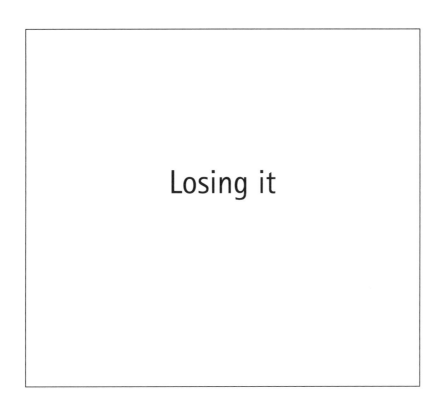

Losing it

How to lose money

"There are three ways of losing money - racing is the quickest, woman are the most pleasant, and farming the most certain."

Lord Amherst

Notable sinkholes

"They bonk three times a day, seven days a week for seven months of the year."

Brian Ketchell, managing director of the collapsed Ostrich Farming Corporation, on the proclivities of his company's main asset (which turned out to be chimerical)

"It would have been cheaper to lower the Atlantic."

Lou Grade, on the failure of the film 'Raise the Titanic'

"This tastes like a fart."

Ross Johnson, then boss of RJR Nabisco, on the tobacco-less cigarette created by his company

"Even Colombian drug barons don't throw that sort of money around without a few signatures."

Merchant banker *on the Nick Leeson Barings fiasco*

"The biggest problem with ITV Digital was the monkey. It confused me - I didn't know if it was the management or the brand."

Kelvin MacKenzie, former editor of the Sun and media pundit

"Marvellous woman by the way - not to bail me out. Like me she believes in free enterprise."

Sir Freddie Laker, on Margaret Thatcher after the collapse of his pioneering low-cost airline

Corporate undertakers

"Heron is a horse with a broken leg. When we saw the cost of fixing the leg, the option of shooting the horse suddenly became much more attractive."

Anonymous banker, commenting on Gerald Ronson's stricken property company

"Insolvency practitioners make their living out of other people's misery and I've always regarded myself as a parasite. But we can't all be surgeons."

Michael Jordan, insolvency expert

"Saving New York from bankruptcy is like making love to a gorilla. You don't stop when you're tired; you stop when he's tired."

Felix Rohatyn

"A remarkable large part of any rescuer's time is taken up in coping with, some would say, fighting off, the very same banks whose money the rescuer is trying to recover."

Lewis Robertson, company doctor

Empty pockets

"Capitalism without bankruptcy is like Christianity without Hell."

Frank Borman, former chief executive of Eastern Air Lines

"I always travel first-class on the train. It's the only way to avoid one's creditors."

Seymour Hicks

"If there is anyone to whom I owe money, I am prepared to forget it if they are."

Errol Flynn

Dying rich

"The man who dies rich, dies disgraced."

Andrew Carnegie, tycoon and philanthropist

"I owe much; I have nothing; the rest I leave to the poor."

Francois Rabelais

"When you have told anyone that you have left him a legacy, the only decent thing to do is die at once."

Samuel Butler

"There's no reason to be the richest man in the cemetery. You can't do any business from there."

Colonel Sanders

"The bottom line? The bottom line is in heaven."

Edwin Land, in reply to an analyst who was badgering him at Polaroid's 1977 AGM about the failure of its cine-camera

Success and failure

Definitions

"Achievement: the death of endeavour and the birth of disgust."

Ambrose Pierce, 'The Devil's Dictionary'

"The successful man is one who makes more than his wife can spend. And the successful woman is one who can find such a man."

Bienvenida Buck, 'How to Marry a Millionaire'

Formulas for success

"I cannot give you the formula for success but I can give you the formula for failure: try to please everybody."

Herbert Bayard Swope

"The secret of life is honesty and fair dealing. If you can fake that, you've got it made."

Groucho Marx

"My formula for success is rise early, work late, and strike oil."

J. Paul Getty

"If you want to be a success in the world, promise everything and deliver nothing."

Napoleon Bonaparte

"The man who can master his time can master nearly anything."

Sir Winston Churchill

"Common sense is not so common."

Voltaire

"You can't learn too soon that the most useful thing about a principle is that it can always be sacrificed to expediency."

W. Somerset Maugham

"Eighty per cent of success is showing up."

Woody Allen

"The trouble with the rat race is that even if you win you're still a rat."

Lily Tomlin

Persistence

"Some succeed because they are destined to, but most succeed because they are determined to."

Anon

"Success is going from failure to failure without loss of enthusiasm."

Sir Winston Churchill

"A man is not finished when he is defeated. He is finished when he quits."

Richard Nixon

"If at first you don't succeed try, try again. Then quit. There's no use being a damn fool about it."

W.C. Fields

Failure

"The minute you start talking about what you're going to do if you lose, you have lost."

George Shultz, statesman and industrialist

"An error doesn't become a mistake unless you fail to learn from it."

Orlando A. Battista

"Man learns little from success, but much from failure."

Arabic proverb

"Failure is both a funny and a sad thing. We worry so much about it coming our way that we cultivate ulcers, nervous breakdowns, tics, rashes or hot flushes. Yet, on the odd occasion when that dark day of doom does come around, we find it isn't really quite as bad as we thought it would be."

G Kingsley Ward, Canadian businessman

"There's always a fear in working class people that all the success and adulation has just been a dream and that you'll wake up tomorrow morning back where you started."

Adam Faith, pop singer and founder of the (alas, defunct) Money Channel

"Show me a good loser and I'll show you a loser."

Paul Newman

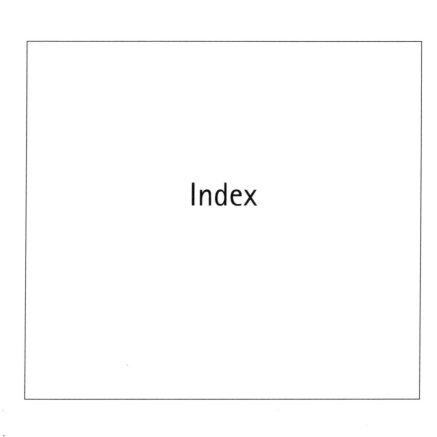

Index

Harriman House Titles

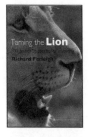

Taming the Lion

100 Secret Strategies for Investing

by Richard Farleigh

Richard Farleigh reveals the 100 secret strategies that he developed to enable him to succeed in the markets.

ISBN: 1897597622, Hardback, 224pp, 2005, Code: 21815, RRP: £12.99
www.harriman-house.com/tamingthelion

The Naked Trader

How anyone can make money trading shares

by Robbie Burns

In this revealing new book, top trader Robbie Burns cuts through the jargon to give you the lowdown on the strategies you need to make money from share dealing.

ISBN: 1897597452, Paperback, 276pp, 2005, Code: 19682, RRP: £12.99
www.harriman-house.com/nakedtrader

Fundology

The Secrets of Successful Fund Investing

by John Chatfeild-Roberts

In this important new book, an award-winning manager at one of the UK's best fund management firms explains in simple language what it takes to buy and sell investment funds successfully

ISBN: 1897597770, Hardback, 166pp, 2006, Code: 22930, RRP: £16.99
www.harriman-house.com/fundology

The Book of Investing Rules

Invaluable advice from 150 master investors

Edited by Philip Jenks and Stephen Eckett

Never before has so much quality advice been packed into a single book. If you want to increase your wealth through investing, this is an unmissable opportunity to acquire knowledge and skills from the best in the world.

ISBN: 1897597215, Paperback, 502pp, 2002, Code: 14870, RRP: £19.99
www.harriman-house.com/rules

The Midas Touch

The strategies that have made Warren Buffett the world's most successful investor

by John Train

This is the book that tells readers how to invest like the man known as 'the Wizard of Omaha' (Forbes) and the investor with 'the Midas Touch'.

ISBN: 1897597290, Hardback, 208pp, 2003, Code: 15842, RRP: £14.00
www.harriman-house.com/midas

Extraordinary Popular Delusions and the Madness of Crowds

by Charles Mackay

Extraordinary Popular Delusions and the Madness of Crowds is often cited as the best book ever written about market psychology. This Harriman House edition includes Charles Mackay's account of the three infamous financial manias - John Law's Mississipi Scheme, the South Sea Bubble, and Tulipomania.

ISBN: 1897597320, Hardback, 96pp, 2003, Code: 16347, RRP: £11.00
www.harriman-house.com/epd

The UK Stock Market Almanac

edited by Stephen Eckett

This Almanac is a unique reference work. Its purpose is to inform, educate and entertain anyone interested in the UK stock market. The structure is based around a 52-week diary, supplemented with articles, facts, figures and trivia, unique to the Harriman House UK Stock Market Almanac.

ISBN: 1897597665, Hardback, 296pp, 2006, Code: 21322, RRP: £19.99
www.harriman-house.com/almanac

Investing with Anthony Bolton

The anatomy of a stock market phenomenon

by Jonathan Davis

This book takes an in-depth look at the way that Bolton goes about his business and analyses in detail the performance of the fund over the past 25 years.

ISBN: 1897597509, Hardback, 176pp, 2004, Code: 20459, RRP: £12.99
www.harriman-house.com/anthonybolton

Harriman House

Harriman House is a specialist publisher of books about money, investing and trading. The books listed are just a few of our titles, and they can all be bought through your local bookshop, direct from www.harriman-house.com or by phone on:

+44 (0)1730 233870

If you would like a copy of our catalogue containing details of all our books, please call us on the same number, email us on enquiries@harriman-house.com, or write to Harriman House, 43 Chapel Street, Petersfield, GU32 3DY. We will send you our latest catalogue by return post.

Global-Investor

Harriman's sister company, Global-Investor, runs the well-known online bookshop of the same name:

www.global-investor.com/bookshop

The Gi Bookshop stocks more than 10,000 titles from over 200 different publishers. We enjoy a reputation for keen prices, friendly service and quick delivery, and have many individual and corporate customers worldwide. Next time you are thinking of buying a finance book, please try us out. We'd like to welcome you as a regular customer.